TREASU

SPIRIT

Tanya Wheway

with Jane Ross-Macdonald

Thorsons

An Imprint of HarperCollins*Publishers*

Thorsons
An Imprint of HarperCollins*Publishers*
77–85 Fulham Palace Road
Hammersmith, London W6 8JB

Published by Thorsons 1998
1 3 5 7 9 10 8 6 4 2

A catalogue record for this book
is available from the British Library

ISBN 0 7225 3770 0

The quotes given in this series of books for the
Mind, Body and Spirit form part of a collection
Tanya Wheway has gathered over many years. For this
reason not all of them are attributed, but the publishers
are anxious to trace any copyright holders that have
not been contacted for permission.

The Sanctuary and the Single Fish Device are the trade mark
of The Sanctuary at Covent Garden Ltd

Text illustrations by Daisy Kelly

Printed and bound in Great Britain by
Woolnoughs Bookbinding Ltd, Irthlingborough, Northants

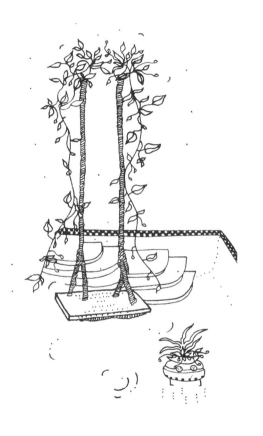

TREASURES FROM THE SANCTUARY

FOR THE

SPIRIT

DEDICATION

I would like to dedicate this set of three books for the mind, body and spirit to my amazingly wonderful family who I love very dearly: husband, business partner and lover, Allan, son Mark and his wife Katherine, daughter Samantha, her husband Jon and grandchildren Emily-Anne and James, also my great parents, Micky and Norman. They have all really made my life totally complete and I would like to thank them for all their love, and also for their understanding and the support they have always given me in respect of all the hours I spend working.

I would like to thank the Sanctuary team for their assistance and support. A very big thank you to Jane Ross-Macdonald for all that she has contributed to the book and for keeping me on track, to Wanda Whitely for opening the doors and being such an inspiration and Nicola Vimpany for her tremendous patience and warm, experienced support.

PREFACE

The Sanctuary in Covent Garden, London, came of age in 1998 as it celebrated its 21st anniversary as a Day Spa exclusively for women. In celebration we have launched this series of *Treasures from the Sanctuary:* one for the *Mind,* one for the *Body* and one for the *Spirit.* We hope they will provide you with words of wisdom and wit to inform, amuse and inspire.

In 1964 an American dancer/choreographer, Gary Cockrell, opened our London premises as the famous Dance Centre, frequented by talented dancers and actors such as Nureyev, Gene Kelly, Dustin Hoffman and Sir John Gielgud. Today the tradition of exercising the body continues with The Sanctuary Fitness Club, exclusively for women.

The Sanctuary philosophy is a holistic one, encompassing mind, body and spirit, which nurtures all the senses. Paintings and candlelight delight the eye, essential oils fragrance the air, fresh produce titillates the taste buds, expert hands pamper the body and the sound of fountains and beautiful music soothe the mind and soul.

INTRODUCTION

What is spirit? In many ways it is indefinable. Our language of words is rich, but some things go beyond language. The word 'spirit' has many different connatations: it is linked with religion, rebellion, courage…

One of the most important uses of the word 'spirit' is its application to the individual. Although it is hard to define what constitutes a person's spirit, it becomes obvious to us when we meet someone whose spirit we truly admire. A person can be attracted to another because of how they look, because of their mind or their personality. However, most truly lasting relationships are built on attraction of the spirit. I believe spirit is the very essence of a person.

> *'I want to travel as far as I can go*
> *I want to reach the joy that's in my soul*
> *And change the limitations that I know*
> *And feel my mind and spirit grow'*

I wish I knew who to attribute this quote to: the four lines say and mean so much. I do hope that our three little books of *Treasures from The Sanctuary*, for the *Mind*, for the *Body* and for the *Spirit* will make a contribution to you achieving the so important elements set out in this quote.

With warmest wishes to you from the Sanctuary Team.

Tanya Wheway
Managing Director
The Sanctuary, Covent Garden

HOW TO USE THIS BOOK

Life is wonderful and precious, but sometimes we are too busy, stressed, angry, upset or grieving to see the beauty that is within ourselves, others and our world. Take a few moments before you get out of bed, whilst travelling to work, having lunch, relaxing or before going to sleep to dip into this little book. See if you can find something that is right for you at this moment: maybe to help you let go of hurts, re-establish your faith, open your mind, improve your relationships with others or get more joy out of living.

I have collected the quotations given in this series of books over many years and I hope you will find them inspirational. The alphabetical listing should make it easy for you to find the subjects that will be of most interest and benefit to you now. However, I hope in time you will read all the books as we can sometimes get out of balance and become too focused on certain aspects of our life whilst neglecting other areas. Our mind, body and spirit are inextricably linked and keeping the three in balance is the key to a full, happy and successful life.

'Acceptance does not preclude change, it precludes remaining in conflict.'

Hugh and Gayle Prather

'God grant me the serenity to accept the things
*   I cannot change*
courage to change the things I can
and wisdom to know the difference.'

Reinhold Niebuhr

ACCEPTANCE

*'I am as my Creator made me, and since He is
satisfied, so am I.'*

Minnie Smith

I am a great believer in the power of positive thinking and
the ability of each of us to change certain situations if we
have the imagination, desire, belief and determination.
However, there are times when it is important to accept
not only that we cannot change things, but that it would
be wiser to leave things as they are.

That said, some people accept negative things in their
lives too readily. Sometimes we should fight for our rights
or the rights of others. A favourite word of mine is balance: we need to accept graciously and with ease when it
is right to do so, and to fight the good fight when it is
appropriate.

'I am only one; but still I am one.
I cannot do everything, but still I can do something.
I will not refuse to do the something I can do.'

Helen Keller

'Troubles are often the tools by which God fashions
us for better things.'

Henry Ward Beecher

ADVERSITY

Adversity comes in many forms, and we all have our own ways of dealing with it. Some resort to head-on confrontations, where both parties get hurt. Others like to blame the nanny state, unemployment, the fast pace of life or the influence of the media – without taking responsibility for their own actions. But we all need to be proactive and responsible: parents, teachers, government, church, police and media.

A few people, such as Helen Keller, display such remarkable spirit in the face of adversity that they provide inspiration for many. She showed that strength of spirit, positive thinking, positive actions and faith can provide the wherewithal to deal with all adversity.

'People do not grow old; when they cease to grow, they become old.'

Ralph Waldo Emerson

'Life can only be understood backwards; it has to be lived forwards.'

Søren Kierkegaard

'Never lose sight of the fact that old age needs so little, but needs that little so much.'

'Age does not protect you from love, but love, to some extent, protects you from age.'

Jeanne Moreau

'It is sad to grow old, but nice to ripen … '

Brigitte Bardot

AGE

Your spirit plays a key role in the way you will age. We all know of elderly people, some very much in the public eye like the Queen Mother, others leading quiet lives, whose spirit we admire and who have inspired us. You can be young at any age if you let your spirit shine through.

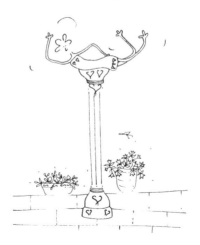

AGGRESSION

'People who fight fire with fire usually end up with ashes.'

Abigail VanBuren

'You cannot shake hands with a clenched fist.'

Indira Gandhi

'When you encounter difficulties and contradictions, do not try to break them, but bend them with gentleness and time.'

'A soft answer turns away anger.'

Aggression should only be used as a last resort. First try tact, charm, persuasion and persistence. If those fail then check how important it is to achieve your aim or to win and what price it is worth paying for this outcome.

'Just to paint is great fun. The colours are lovely to look at and delicious to squeeze out. Matching them, however crudely, with what you see is fascinating and absolutely absorbing. Try it if you have not done so – before you die.'

Winston Churchill

'When I get to heaven I mean to spend a considerable portion of my first million years in painting, and so get to the bottom of the subject.'

Winston Churchill

'Art is the only way to run away without leaving home.'

Twyla Tharp

ART

You do not have to be an artist to paint or draw, just as you do not need to be a writer to write. Within all of us is a deep sense of creativity, a desire to express what we see and feel in ways other than words. Art therapy is used in special schools and with patients who have experienced a great shock as a way of drawing out non-verbal expression and coming to terms with sadness, guilt or loss. It is also a marvellously contemplative activity which will absorb you for hours, take you away from your petty daily concerns and even get you in touch with nature. So if you haven't thought of putting brush to paper since primary school, think again. Books, evening and weekend courses can be a great way to get started. A visit to your local craft shop is another way to stimulate yourself into action. Visiting local exhibitions and national museums and galleries can also nurture and stimulate your mind and spirit.

'People see God every day; they just don't recognize him.'

Pearl J. Bailey

'We are caught in the contradiction of finding life a rather perplexing puzzle which causes us a lot of misery, and at the same time being dimly aware of the boundless, limitless nature of life. So we begin looking for an answer to the puzzle.'

Charlotte Joko Beck

'In contemporary America people are again discovering how to drink from their own wells.'

Lynn R. Lawrence

'Awareness is the key. When I know what I am doing, I have the option to change.'

Anne Wilson Schaef

AWARENESS

Opening our minds, allowing ourselves to be inquisitive and intuitive enables us to grow. Our awareness should not just be aimed at the external, but also at the internal: getting in touch with our own spirit, the essence of our being. Stillness, reflection, meditation and prayer can lead us to a greater awareness, but sometimes it is an activity or experience that suddenly opens a door to greater understanding, adding a new dimension to our lives.

'Maintain the body, develop the mind, and nourish the spirit to create a whole balanced person.'

Jack Clarke

'I don't want to get to the end of my life and find that I have just lived the length of it. I want to have lived the width of it as well.'

Diane Ackerman

BALANCE

Balance is the key to success in all things. Do not neglect your mind, body or spirit. Invest time and energy in all of them equally – it will be the best investment you ever make, not just for this life but for whatever is to follow.

'Every time you breathe in, thank a tree.'

John Wright

'Listen to the air
You can hear it, feel it
Smell it, taste it.'

John Lame Deer

BREATHING

We can last for days without food or water, but deprived of breath we are deprived of life. Yet most of us do not breathe correctly. Breathing techniques are a crucial part of many spiritual disciplines, for correct breathing promotes healthy elimination of toxins from the body, improves circulation, increases energy, can help disperse emotional tension and promote a sense of stillness and peace. Notice how when you are tense, worried or frightened your breathing becomes short and shallow, and when you are relaxed in mind and body it becomes calm and full. Try the breathing exercises overleaf whenever you want to relax.

Breathing Exercise I

1. Close the right nostril gently with one finger.
2. Breathe in through the left nostril.
3. Close your left nostril.
4. Hold your breath for a moment, then release the right nostril.
5. Breathe out through the right nostril, then in.
6. Close both nostrils for a moment before releasing the left nostril and exhaling.
7. Repcat 6 times.

Breathing Exercise II

1 Lie down in a comfortable place.
2 Ensure your body is lying evenly, with your hands by your sides and your palms facing upwards.
3 Close your eyes and feel the stillness.
4 Inhale and exhale fully, feeling your abdomen rise and fall.
5 As you inhale, repeat 'Deep and long and slow,' and as you exhale, repeat 'Slow and long and deep.' Notice how your breathing becomes deeper, longer and slower.
6 Feel your inhalations taking in energy and your exhalations breathing out stress.
7 After five minutes or so, stir yourself gently.

'Laugh. Laughter is immeasurable. Be joyful though you have considered all the facts.'

Wendell Berry

CELEBRATE

Participating in someone else's joy is an uplifting experience: take every opportunity you can to celebrate life passages, social events, happy occasions. Even funerals can be a time for joy and celebration if the dead person has lived a long and full life.

We tend to suppress our emotions, whether they be happy or sad. Don't let one day run into another and the weeks become months without a celebration of some kind taking place fairly frequently. If you seek you will invariably find something to celebrate. Going to a church or other place of worship once a week to give thanks for all the good things in life can be one form of celebration, as can saying a short prayer of thanksgiving before starting a meal.

CHAKRAS

In oriental medicine the body has seven focal points where energy is centred, called chakras.

The root chakra is at the base of the spine and is connected with our 'rootedness' to the earth, survival and security.

The sacral chakra is in the pelvic area and is associated with sexuality and emotions.

The solar plexus chakra is just below the sternum and is connected with power and self-confidence.

The heart chakra is in the centre of the body level with the heart, and is associated with love and friendship.

The throat chakra is in the middle of the throat area and is to do with communication and creativity.

The brow chakra is in between the eyebrows and concerns the intellect and imagination.

The crown chakra is on the top of our head and is associated with spirituality and beauty.

These areas can be useful aids when meditating if you feel any one area needs to be boosted. Concentrate on the chakra and feel energy, warmth and colour radiating outwards from the point. The chakras are also associated with the colours of the rainbow, where root is red, sacral is orange, solar plexus is yellow, and so on. Healers will use their sense of the colours of your aura to tune into areas that need work.

CHANGE

'Change and challenge – the ecstasy of movement and the dance.'

Ralph Metzner

There was an 86 year old man who realized that in order to get more out of life he didn't have to change the world – the world was already beautiful. Instead what he had to do was to change himself.

The only constant in life is change. Nothing is forever. Most people resent, fear or resist change, but we must learn to expect change, to accept and positively embrace it, and to actively look for the opportunities and good things that it can bring. *See Letting Go p81.*

1 Take a moment to remember past life-changes that came as a shock and past hurts that you thought at the time would never heal, and realize how time has gradually helped.

2 On a sheet of paper, head two columns 'if only' and 'what is'.

3 In dealing with the pain of change, fill in your feelings under the 'if only' column.

4 In the 'what is' column, note down the current state of reality.

5 Turn over the page and write 'what now?' – the answers will enable you to move forwards.

*'Character is like the foundation of a house …
it is below the surface.'*

'To be interesting, we need to be interested.'

*'When a happy person enters the room, it's as if
another candle has been lighted.'*

*'Neither speak well nor ill of yourself. If well, people
will not believe you; if ill, they will believe a great
deal more than you say.'*

CHARACTER

Take care of your mind and spirit, for they form your character, from which develops your integrity, will and personality.

'A real character': sometimes we use the word to describe someone who is unusual or entertaining, and thank goodness for characters – they remove the blandness that can otherwise prevail. Be careful of knocking the character out of the people we love, and encourage its development (as long as it is not destructive).

Each person is made up of all the genes they have inherited and the experiences they have had through life: good and bad. These, together with the individual's own will, have formed their character. Spend some time getting to know and understand the character you have become, what has led you to become the person you are today and what, if anything, you would like to change.

CHILDREN

'Your children are not your children.
They are the sons and daughters of Life's longing
*   for itself*
They come through you but not from you.
And though they are with you yet they belong not
*   to you…*
You may strive to be like them, but seek not to make
*   them like you.*
For life goes not backward nor tarries with
*   yesterday.'*

                    From Kahlil Gibran, *The Prophet*

'You may have tangible wealth untold;
Caskets of jewels and coffers of gold.
Richer than I you can never be –
I have a mother who read to me.'

                    Strickland Gillilan

CHOICES

'We cannot direct the wind but we can adjust the sails.'

We make choices every day about how to live our lives. About whether to give or take pleasure. About whether to be courageous or timid; to see the glass as half full or half empty; to be proactive or lazy. Your life has not just been dumped on you; it has been fashioned daily by you according to the choices you have made. Even if you are going through a difficult time or facing personal tragedy you still have a choice about how to react to the events in your life. Your thoughts are crucial: positive thoughts radiate healthy, life-giving energy; negative thoughts are damaging and disempowering.

'Christmas is a time for children, no matter what
their age.
Spirit is the only ticket, and heart the only gauge.'

CHRISTMAS

Christmas should be the most wonderful time to spend with those we love. Time to relax, to share, to have fun and to celebrate the birth of Jesus. Very sadly the reverse is often true. There are more divorces filed immediately after Christmas than at any other time of the year. Commercialization, advertising, and pressures of our own making are major stressors at this time of year. Shopping, wrapping, planning, cooking, entertaining, travelling to family, and high expectations all add to the pressures.

Plan and prepare well ahead, delegate so that everyone is encouraged to contribute and 'martyrdom' is avoided. Allow some time for worship, walking, relaxation and fun. Have a family get-together a couple of months ahead and discuss what you will each do to make the festivities a success, and to make sure you all remember what the spirit of Christmas is really about.

'Annihilating all that's made to a green thought in a green shade.'

Andrew Marvell

COLOUR HEALING

Colours vibrate at different frequencies, and research has shown that they can profoundly affect our mind, body and spiritual well-being. Use the colours you need in clothes, food and in your environment…

Red: for confidence and help in overcoming depression
Orange: lifts the spirits and gives a feeling of energy
Yellow: for assisting self-control and optimism
Green: for balancing the mind and easing stress
Turquoise: works on the immune system
Blue: for peace and quiet
Indigo: calms anger
Violet: calms mental disturbance and builds confidence

'God has given us two ears, two eyes, but only one tongue. We should hear and see more than we speak.'

'Computers are useless. They can only give you answers.'

Pablo Picasso

'If you think twice before you speak once, you will speak better for it.'

'Speech is a beautiful net in which souls are caught.'

'Some people talk simply because they think sound is more manageable than silence.'

Margaret Halsey

COMMUNICATION

Communication is so important but so difficult to get right, and our daily lives are filled with minor misunderstandings arising from lack of effective communication. Of course we know we communicate not simply by talking, but by our body language, the way in which we listen, our tone of voice and the type of words we use. Sometimes it pays to be a little more creative in our communication:

- Send a card or write a letter.
- Write a poem or song.
- Send some flowers.
- Put your message on tape, or even a video.

If you are serious about improving the quality of your relationships, both at home and at work, there are many worthwhile books and courses on communication.

'I heard a story about a man who went about the countryside asking people how they would spend their last day on earth. He came upon a woman who was out hoeing her garden, surrounded by her children and a neighbour. He decided he might as well ask her too, even though he didn't expect much of an answer. "Woman," he asked, "if this were your last day on earth, if tomorrow it was certain you would die, what would you do today?" "Oh," she said, "I would go on hoeing my garden and taking care of my children and talking to my neighbour."'

Sue Monk Kidd

'There are two things to aim at in life: first, to get what you want; and after that, to enjoy it. Only the wisest of mankind achieve the second.'

Logan Pearsall Smith

'From contentment with little comes happiness.'

African proverb

CONTENTMENT

Contentment must not be confused with complacency. Contentment does not mean that you no longer have things to do, places to go, people to see and a great deal more to achieve in your life; what it does mean is feeling 'centred', on good terms with yourself and appreciative of what, where and who you are *now*.

CONTRIBUTING TO SOCIETY

*'If you yourself would feel fine, heal and serve and
give from time to time.'*

Native American proverb

*'You cannot help people permanently by doing
for them what they should do for themselves.'*

*'If you want to feel good about yourself, do good
things.'*

John-Roger

'It is better to give than to receive.'

By absorbing yourself in the problems and trials of another
you can often find a sense of personal empowerment.
To do voluntary work, to donate your time to a charitable
organization or to help others in any small way can take
you out of yourself in a refreshing and challenging way.

COUNT YOUR BLESSINGS

*'If I give all I possess to the poor and surrender my
body to the flames but have not love, I gain nothing.'*
Corinthians

*'Behold, I'm alive. On what?
Neither childhood nor future grows less …
Surplus of existence is welling up in my heart.'*
Rainer Maria Rilke

'I thank you god for most this amazing day'
e. e. cummings

It's a familiar enough saying, but how many of us actually do
it? On a clean sheet of paper, take the time to write down all
those people, possessions, talents, physical and emotional
attributes, and experiences you are thankful for. Keep it safe
and look over it from time to time for energy and inspiration.

COURAGE

Courage is a matter of seeing things in perspective, tapping into the strength that lies within us, having belief in ourself and faith in a divine power. Too much thinking can often zap our power, leading us into complex 'what if' scenarios. First we need to decide the importance of the task or challenge ahead, ask ourselves the price we are willing to pay, and, if the green light is still there – grit your teeth and go for it!

'Courage is the price that life exacts for granting peace.'

Amelia Earhart

'Do not follow where the path might lead ... go instead where there is no path and leave a trail.'

'When we face our fears and let ourselves know our connection to the power that is in us and beyond us, we learn courage.'

Anne Wilson Schaef

'Come to the edge.
We might fall.
Come to the edge.
It's too high.
COME TO THE EDGE!
And they came,
And he pushed ...
And they flew!'

Christopher Logue

CRITICISM

*'He has the right to criticize who has the heart
to help.'*

Abraham Lincoln

'If Jesus Christ were to come today, people would not even crucify him. They would ask him to dinner, and hear what he had to say, and make fun of it.'
Thomas Carlyle

'I dreamed death came the other night, and
    Heaven's gate swung wide.
With kindly grace, an angel fair ushered me inside.
And there to my astonishment, stood folks I'd known
    on earth,
Some I'd judged and labelled as "unfit", "of little
    worth",
Indignant words rose to my lips, but never were
    set free,
For every face showed stunned surprise: no-one
    expected me!'

'A fault once denied is twice committed.'

'Those afraid of dying die a thousand deaths.'

*'Earth brings us to life and nourishes us
Earth takes us back again.
Birth and death are present in every moment.'*
Thich Nhat Hanh

*'Once you accept your own death all of a sudden
you are free to live. You no longer care about your
reputation, you no longer care except so far as your
life can be used tactically – to promote a cause you
believe in.'*

Saul Alinsky

*'There's still so much I'd like to see, so much to
learn, and death is just around the corner. Not
that that worries me. On the contrary, it is no more
than passing from one room to another. But there's
a difference for me, you know. Because in that other
room I shall be able to see.'*
Helen Keller

DEATH

I find it a comforting thought to know that death happens to all of us – the wealthiest, the most beautiful, the most intelligent and the most holy. I also find it comforting to know that I have lived a full, happy and productive life, and that I have made my contribution to the continuance of the human race by leaving the precious lives of my children and grandchildren to live on after me. I do believe that our spirit lives on in some form, but while we are still here we need to be sure that we truly *live* the life we do have: live it and enjoy it day by day.

DREAMING

'You know, there's a dream dreaming us.'

'Dreaming hitches the soul to the stars.'

'The future belongs to those who believe in the beauty of their dreams.'

Eleanor Roosevelt

FAITH

*'We must never lose faith in human nature –
there is nowhere else to go.'*

Katrina Graham

*'Without faith a man can do nothing: with it all
things are possible.'*

Sir William Osler

*'Doubting is not a sin. Nor does it denote a lack of
faith … Doubting is an invitation to enter into the
mystery more deeply.'*

John Aurelio

Faith is a powerful and wonderful thing to have: not just
religious faith, but faith in ourselves, faith in our loved ones,
and faith in the human race. Our faith will be tried and test-
ed, probably many times in our lives, but it is important to
be able to bounce back and rebuild our faith if it sometimes
fails us. Strength of faith will attract good things to us, while
loss of faith leads us down a path of negativity.

FEELINGS

'Noble deeds and hot baths are the best cures for depression.'

Dodie Smith

'When the spirits sink too low, the best cordial is to read over all the letters of one's friends.'

William Shenstone

'Those who do not know how to weep with their whole heart don't know how to laugh either.'

Golda Meir

God gave us many different feelings, and there is nothing wrong with any of them in the right place at the right time. Anger helps us muster the power to right wrongs; grief and the mourning process help us deal with loss and pain. But do not hold on to these feelings for too long – like holding a piece of burning coal, the only person it burns is you.

FENG SHUI

Just as the Chinese believed there were channels of energy running through our bodies, called meridians, so too they built a system of planning and designing a living space, based on the idea that there are energy channels passing through landscapes and houses. Feng Shui literally means 'wind and water' and is a natural, earth-conscious system for living in harmony with our environment. Today, many buildings in the Far East are designed with the aid of a feng shui master, and the art is also growing in popularity in the West. There are many books now on the subject that will help you re-design your home to eliminate any negative aspects which might be affecting your relationships, your job or your children. Much of it is common sense: eliminating clutter, avoiding blocking passages, allowing in light and air – but there are more complex elements which enter the realm of spirituality and for which you may need to suspend disbelief. I do recommend an open mind and a willingness to see how feng shui may add positive energy to your life.

'To err is human, to forgive infrequent.'

'He who forgives ends the quarrel.'

'Forgiveness may be the greatest healer.'
John-Roger and Peter McWilliams

'Many people start by being unable to forgive another person and end up being unable to forgive themselves. At least whilst the other person is still alive one has the opportunity to avoid the latter.'
Tanya Wheway

'A former inmate of a Nazi concentration camp was visiting a friend who had shared the ordeal with him. "Have you forgiven the Nazis?" he asked his friend. "Yes." "Well, I haven't. I'm still consumed with hatred for them." "In that case," said his friend gently, "they still have you in a prison."'
Antony de Mello

FORGIVENESS

I really do detest waste: being unable to forgive and move on is such a waste of precious time. I see so many people eaten up with anger, grudges, resentments and other destructive feelings. Remember, no one is perfect.

If you leave it too long to forgive, it may well be too late: now is the very best time. Forgiving and forgetting are two different things: we can and should forgive, but everything that happens to us is kept on record … that is just the way it is, so it is reasonable not to forget. But let it go. A useful exercise is to say, 'I forgive …' again and again, even if you don't at first believe you do. Do it for your own sake if for no other reason. Put things into perspective and build something positive from your experience.

'I always felt that the great high privilege, relief and comfort of friendship was that one had to explain nothing.'

Katherine Mansfield

'A false friend and a shadow attend only when the sun shines.'

'Instead of loving your enemies, why don't you treat your friends a little better?'

'Most pathfinders carry a little secret: they are not entirely alone. Someone else takes their dreams and illusions, their good times and bad times, their triumphs and defeats, almost as seriously as they themselves do.'

Gail Sheehy

FRIENDSHIP

How many of us have become so busy that we no longer have time for friends? We write just at Christmas, we rarely phone and we have to make an appointment in our diary if we are to find time to meet: at best this time is treated as a luxury and at worst resented. Resolve to contact one friend or family member a day for the next month: a friendly call, quick e-mail or postcard will do – and then make it a habit.

GARDENS

'If you want to be happy for a few hours, drink wine.
If you want to be happy for three days, get married.
If you want to be happy for eight days, kill your pig and eat it.
And if you want to be happy for ever, get a garden.'
Chinese proverb

'The Kiss of the sun for pardon,
The song of the birds for mirth,
One is nearer God's Heart in a garden
Than anywhere else on earth.'
Dorothy Frances Gurney

GOALS

'Find an aim in life before you run out of ammunition.'

'It is good to have an end to journey towards; but it is the journey that matters in the end.'

Ursula K. Le Guin

Reaching your goal is but a moment in time. Goals give purpose and direction to our lives and they stretch and motivate us, but they should not be the 'be all and end all'. The goal is just a station you arrive at, the journey is where you have spent most of your time, so remember to savour the moments along the way.

'We look not to the things that are seen, but to the things that are unseen, for the things that are seen are transient, the things that are unseen are eternal.'
Napoleon Hill

'If only God would give me some clear sign! Like making a large deposit in my name at a Swiss Bank.'
Woody Allen

'And if you would know God, be not therefore a solver of riddles. Rather look about you and you shall see Him playing with your children. And look into space; you shall see Him walking in the cloud, outstretching His arms in the lightning and descending rain. You shall see Him smiling in flowers, then rising and waving His hands in trees.'

Kahlil Gibran

GOD

I used to like the way Dave Allen finished his shows: 'May your God go with you.' My personal approach and belief is not concerned with a name. I am sure there is a lot more to us than just a mind and a body, and I believe that the other essential part of us goes beyond the here and now. What I have absolutely no idea about is the form that part takes. For me the key ingredients for living our lives are:

- To value and use the gifts we have received (life, time, abilities, attributes, senses) as wisely and well as we can.
- To have a positive impact upon the lives of those with whom we come into contact in the course of our journey through life.
- To respect and honour the world we live in.
- To give love, support and, where appropriate, guidance to our families.
- To make each day a celebration of life and an appropriate preparation for the life to come.

'Grief is itself a medicine.'

William Cowper

'We are healed of suffering only by experiencing it to the full.'

Marcel Proust

*'Too mourn too long for those we love is self-
        indulgent
But to honour their memory with a promise
To live a little better for having known them
Gives purpose to their life and an easier acceptance
        of their death.'*

GRIEF

There was a time when it was felt that prescribing drugs such as Valium and Librium to people in distress was useful for tiding them over the first few weeks of grief. Now doctors and counsellors have learned that the grieving process – shock/denial, anger/depression, understanding/ acceptance – should not be suppressed or denied, but lived through in a natural way. It is natural to feel sad, angry and cheated at this time. We need to experience and embrace our grief, and then, in time, let it go. *See Death p43 and Letting Go p81.*

*'In some Islamic societies you would never bring
a sick person flowers and candies as we do in this
country. Instead, you would tell them a story of
patience, endurance and triumph. The images
such a tale would plant in their awareness would
circulate through their souls just as powerfully as
a medicinal elixir would travel to the diseased cells
by way of the blood-stream. The more the story is
considered, the more it can empower the body's own
healing mechanisms.'*

Richard Stone

*'The best physicians are Dr Diet, Dr Quiet and
Dr Merryman.'*

HEALTH

I believe that our 'inner wisdom' knows, at a fundamental level, what ails us and what we must do to rectify the condition, and I am vastly encouraged to see the shift which is taking place in health care towards integrating complementary medicine with orthodox Western medicine. We are moving towards a holistic approach to health in which the mind, body and spirit are integrated and in balance. And when these are in balance our immune system and self-healing powers work more effectively.

HOPE

'You don't seem to realize that a poor person who is
unhappy is in a better position than a rich person
who is unhappy. Because the poor person has hope.
He thinks money would help.'

Jean Kerr

'Hope is the thing with feathers
That perches in the soul –
And sings the tune without words
And never stops – at all.'

Emily Dickinson

'Hope for the best, get ready for the worst, and then
take what God chooses to send.'

'We need hope to keep us going, but not if it stops us from actively doing something to move forward to what it is we are hoping for.'

IMAGINATION

'A mind once stretched by a new idea never gains its original dimensions.'

'Imagination is more important than knowledge.'
Albert Einstein

'He said he should prefer not to know the sources of the Nile, and that there should be some unknown regions preserved as hunting grounds for the poetic imagination.'

George Eliot

Children have such wonderful imaginations, but they are often stifled and discouraged both at home and school. The imagination unleashes our creative powers, helps our intuitive abilities to function more effectively and widens our horizons.

'Genius is one percent inspiration and ninety-nine percent perspiration.'

'So many people don't know how to inspire themselves. Use everything that moves you: music, walking by water, flowers ... Inspiration helps so deeply in overcoming laziness, summons what the Sufis call "the fragrance of the Beloved" into everything.'

Andrew Harvey

'Inspiration is the gentle listening to the wisdom of our inner being.'

Anne Wilson Schaef

INSPIRATION

Inspiration cannot be forced. Sometimes it simply comes like a bolt out of the blue; at other times it totally refuses to come out to play. There are times, however, when we can cajole it into action by freeing our minds – listening to some beautiful music, spending time in a beautiful garden, meditating, reading, exposing ourselves to a new environment or spending time with positive, passionate and creative people.

'We make a living by what we get. We make a life by what we give.'

'The real character of a person is measured by what they do when no one is looking.'

'He put the power of love before the love of power, and I loved him for that.'

Madame Sadat

'Don't compromise yourself. You are all you've got.'

Janis Joplin

'It's important that people know what you stand for. It's equally important that they know what you won't stand for.'

Mary Waldrop

'This above all – to thine own self be true,'

Shakespeare

INTEGRITY

Do unto others as you would have them do unto you is a pretty good rule to go by. Integrity is a wonderful bedfellow. It is great to be able to retire at night and sleep the sleep of the innocent knowing that your integrity is intact. But remember that your integrity is not just to do with what you have done, but also what you have left undone or allowed to continue.

'There are more things in heaven and earth,
    Horatio,
Than are dreamt of in your philosophy.'

Shakespeare

'Go where your heart leads you.'

'It is sometimes frightening to trust my intuition.
It is always disastrous not to.'

Anne Wilson Schaef

INTUITION

'Gut' feelings, 'vibes', a 'sixth sense': they are so often proved right, but our lives tend to be so ruled by science and technology that it is easy to lose touch with that little voice within us. Many down-to-earth people, living very normal lives, do have experiences which seem inexplicable, even verging on the mystical. Some people call them no more than coincidences, whereas others refer to them as 'supernatural' occurrences. They often happen when we allow our intuitive selves to come to the fore, when we allow our consciousness to expand in new directions.

Throughout history and across cultures, rituals and vision quests have been conducted to allow those suffering from disease or serious crises the opportunity to access what we now might call 'inner wisdom'. Yoga and meditation and finding your own 'spiritual path' can also help you raise your consciousness in this way.

'Joy has the power to open our hearts, remove fear, instill hope, and foster healing.'

Charlotte Davis Kasl

'No wonder life has seemed dull at times – we have made it that way. It's not that the potential for joy wasn't there. We were just too busy and controlling to notice it.'

Anne Wilson Schaef

'Surely the strange beauty of the world must somewhere rest on pure joy.'

Louise Bogan

'Joy is the holy fire that keeps our purpose warm and our intelligence aglow.'

Helen Keller

JOY

Spontaneity and joy often go hand in hand. Work overload, taking ourselves too seriously, becoming too routine-bound, cynicism, busy-ness ... all make it nigh impossible for us to experience the bliss and wonderment of joy. Let the pure joy of living come into your life every day, and use your senses to pick up on the positive and beautiful things around you. We all have a choice: we can get up in the morning and spend the day finding fault with the world and focusing on the unpleasant things around us, or we can choose to focus on the wonderful things. It's up to you. If you want to find more joy in your life, start to live life *as if* you were joyful. This in turn will breed its own joy, and in time you won't have to make any effort, it will just happen.

♥ Take some time out to listen to some beautiful music.
♥ Commune with nature.
♥ Take a small child to the zoo, fair or circus.
♥ Just enjoy the joy of being.

JUDGING

'Judge not lest ye be judged.'

The Bible

'Don't judge a tree till you see the fruit.'

'If I could see what's going on with myself as well as I see what's going on with others, I'd be fixed by now.'

'In a world that constantly asks us to make up our minds about other people, a non-judgmental presence seems nearly impossible. But it is one of the most beautiful fruits of a deep spiritual life.'

Henri J. M. Nouwen

KARMA

'Do unto others as you would have them do to you.'

'Life is not a having and a getting but a being and a becoming.'

Matthew Arnold

The concept of Karma, a fundamental element of Buddhism and Hinduism, is essentially cause and effect. Our actions will cause corresponding reactions. Almost every religion has some variation on the theme of 'for as you sow, so shall you reap'. This is easy enough to understand in the physical world, but some Eastern religions believe that the power resulting from an individual's acts will determine that person's cycle of reincarnations before they attain release from this world. The sum total of the acts done during one stage of a person's existence will determine their destiny in the next.

'Kind words can be short and easy to speak, but their echoes are truly endless.'

Mother Teresa

'Let no one come to you without leaving better and happier, be the living expression of God's kindness, kindness in your face, kindness in your heart, kindness in your smile.'

Mother Teresa

'Better do a kindness at home than walk a thousand miles to burn incense.'

'My religion is very simple. My religion is kindness.'

The Dalai Lama

'Three things in human life are important. The first is to be kind, the second is to be kind and the third is to be kind.'

Henry James

KINDNESS

Friendships are fostered by kindness. Friendships offer hope and support, comfort and companionship. They are the lights that can sometimes guide you to the end of your tunnel. Do not isolate yourself from the joy and healing power of friendship, and don't be afraid of asking for support when you need it. Remember also that friendship is about giving as well as receiving, and little acts of kindness are incredibly important.

'Knowledge is folly unless grace guides it.'

*'Beware you be not swallowed up in books! An
ounce of love is worth a pound of knowledge.'*
John Wesley

*'Integrity without knowledge is weak and useless,
and knowledge without integrity is dangerous and
dreadful.'*

Samuel Johnson

KNOWLEDGE

The issue is not so much having knowledge; but more how that knowledge is used. It can be used for personal power or to share, and it can be used for good or evil. It can be wasted or it can be used in a profound way, the ripples of which may affect the future of humanity. Computerization, weapons of destruction and genetic engineering are all possible threats to mankind, yet we cannot absolve ourselves of responsibility. If we want to see that this kind of knowledge is used positively on behalf of humanity and not against it we need to 'get off our butts' and become players. Read, listen, look, ask questions, vote, support, and encourage children to take an interest and participate.

There is again a point of balance when it comes to acquiring knowledge. Even if you studied the whole of your life there would still be a tremendous amount you would not know. Although knowledge is a wonderful thing and can be extremely useful, life is about living, not just studying.

LEARNING

*'After a while you learn the difference between holding a
    hand and chaining a soul.
And you learn that love doesn't mean security.
You begin to learn that kisses aren't contracts and presents
    aren't promises
And you begin to accept your defeats with your head up
    and eyes open,
And with the grace of an adult, not the grief of a child.
You learn to build all your roads on today,
Because tomorrow's ground is too uncertain for your plans.
After a while you learn that even sunshine burns if you
    get too much.
So plant your own garden and decorate your own soul
Instead of waiting for someone to bring you flowers.
You will learn that you really can endure,
That you really are special
And that you really do have worth.
So live to learn and know yourself.
In doing so you will learn to live.'*

Anon

'To everything there is a season, a time for every purpose under the sun.'

Ecclesiastes

*'Within the circles of our lives
we dance the circles of the years.'*

Wendell Berry

'When the heart weeps for what it has lost, the spirit laughs for what it has found.'

Sufi proverb

'We cannot change the past, but we can take the good things from it and move on.'

Tanya Wheway

'We must be willing to get rid of the life we've planned, so as to have the life that is waiting for us. The old skin has to be shed before the new one can come.'

Joseph Campbell

LETTING GO

A Zen Master asked a group of Westerners what they thought was the most important word in the English language. They suggested words such as love, truth, failure. He replied, 'No, it's a three letter word, "let". Let it be. Let it happen …'

This also applies to 'let it go'. There is always a time to let go and move on. Nothing is for ever. Everything is constantly moving and changing. There are only two things in life that we can be certain of – one is death and the other is change. If we can learn to accept and embrace change, then it becomes a little easier to accept and a little less painful when it happens. Think of the cycles of the seasons, and how things die and are renewed with time. We're always having to let go, whether it's of our children who grow up, of possessions or job, our youth, a loved one. But the loss leaves space for other good things: they may not be the same as those you have lost, but in their own way they may be special and rewarding.

LIFE'S LESSONS

'To see the greatness of a mountain, one must keep one's distance.'

Lama Govinda

'I think that wherever your journey takes you, there are new gods waiting there with divine patience – and laughter.'

Susan Watkins

'Teachers open the door, but you enter by yourself.'

'Mistakes are part of the dues one pays for a full life.'

Sophia Loren

'In youth we learn; with age we understand.'
Marie Ebner-Eschenbach

'Keep learning about the world ... Use your mind to the hilt. Life passes quickly and, towards the end, gathers speed like a freight train running downhill. The more you know, the more you enrich yourself and others.'

Susan Trott

'In the end, everyone is our teacher, on one level or another. The child is our teacher, our friends, our family, the stranger on the street. Every experience is a challenge; a teaching is always hidden in it. Every thought that bubbles up in our minds can teach us things about ourselves, if we are able to listen.'

David A. Cooper

LISTENING

'It is as though he listened and such listening as his enfolds us in a silence in which at last we begin to hear what we are meant to be.'

Lao Tse

'When the body is finally listened to ... It becomes eloquent. It's like changing a fiddle into a Stradivarius.'

Look and you will see, listen and you will hear! Being still and really listening to our minds, our bodies and our soul will enable us to get in tune with them, and through a greater understanding of them be able to nurture them better.

When someone is speaking to you, do them the courtesy of giving them your undivided attention, or ask if you can be excused until you are able to devote your time properly to them.

LIVING

*'Accept the pain, cherish the joys, resolve the regrets;
then can come the best of benediction – "If I had my
life to live over, I'd do it all the same".'*

Joan McIntosh

*'I like living. I have sometimes been wildly,
despairingly, acutely miserable, racked with sorrow,
but through it all I still know, quite certainly, that
just to be alive is a grand thing.'*

Agatha Christie

*'To live is the rarest thing in the world. Most people
exist, that is all.'*

Oscar Wilde

*'What a wonderful life I've had! I only wish I'd
realized it sooner.'*

Colette

'Trouble is part of your life, and if you don't share it,
you don't give the person who loves you enough
chance to love you enough.'

Diana Shore

'Love is a fruit in season at all times.'

Mother Teresa

LOVE

'Love is the only thing that we can carry with us
when we go, and it makes the end so easy.'

Louisa May Alcott

'We are all born for love. It is the principle of
existence, and its only end.'

Disraeli

'Love is life – creation, seed and leaf
and blossom and fruit and seed, love is growth
and search and reach and touch and dance.
Love is nurture and succour and feed and pleasure,
love is pleasuring ourselves pleasuring each other,
love is life believing in itself.'

Manitongquat

'Those who have never known the deep intimacy
and intense companionship of mutual love have
missed the best thing that life has to give.'

Bertrand Russell

MANTRAS

Every sound has a resonance, or vibration, that affects the mind and body in ways that can be positive or negative. Mantras are sacred words or sounds that are repeated many times, for example during meditation, and have a relaxing or devotional effect. Familiar mantras are 'om', 'peace', 'calm', 'aah', and constant repetition helps clear your mind of distracting thoughts and allow you to feel a connection between yourself and a higher power.

'… let there be spaces in your togetherness.
And let the winds of the heavens dance between you.
Love one another, but make not a bond of love:
Let it rather be a moving sea between the shores of
*   your souls.'*

From Kahlil Gibran, *The Prophet*

MARRIAGE

Any relationship, including marriage, benefits both from spending 'quality time' together, and from developing your own interests outside the relationship. It is incredibly important to remember that you cannot 'un-say' or 'un-do' anything: each time you say or do anything negative or hurtful the 'rock' of your relationship will get chipped away. The keys to successful, loving partnerships are:

- ♥ mutual respect for each other's strengths
- ♥ acceptance of each other's weaknesses
- ♥ frequently giving compliments and positive feedback
- ♥ enthusiam for giving as well as joy in receiving, including sexually.
- ♥ honesty and an ability to communicate and listen
- ♥ working together on problems, challenges and planning the future
- ♥ keeping romance alive, avoiding ruts and routines, being creative and actively pursuing spontaneity.

MEDITATION

'Sitting quietly, doing nothing,
Spring comes and the grass grows by itself.'

Taoist poem

'Within you is a stillness and a sanctuary to which
you can retreat at any time and be yourself.'

Herman Hesse, *Siddhartha*

'You don't have to do anything to find the Self –
you have to stop doing anything … Nothing is more
important for humanity today than for everyone
to understand that he can easily reach this state.'

Deepak Chopra

'Too much metal
Too much fat
Too many jokes
Not enough meditation …'

Allen Ginsberg

Meditation is a way of controlling and stilling the chattering of thought patterns constantly rushing through our minds. Meditation can help us clear and relax our minds so that when we return to activity we can be more focused and effective. It can enhance our immune system, lower blood pressure and combat the harmful effects of stress on our bodies. On a spiritual level it can enable us to experience a timeless, spaceless realm on the path to enlightenment.

Meditation I

1 Sit in a quiet room in a comfortable position with your eyes closed.
2 Place your hands on your abdomen.
3 Breathe in and out slowly, concentrating on the breath.
4 Notice how the air flows in and out, and the slight pause between each inhalation and exhalation.
5 Feel your lungs as they fill and your abdomen as it rises and falls.
6 Be conscious of the life force that is allowing you to breathe involuntarily.

Meditation II
1 Sit in a quiet room in a comfortable position with your eyes closed.
2 Bring to mind someone who cares or who cared for you deeply and unconditionally.
3 Feel yourself surrounded by their love and support.
4 Take in the love with every breath you take, expanding with it and embracing it.
5 Know that you are worth it.

Meditation III
1 Sit in a quiet room in a comfortable position with your eyes closed.
2 With every out breath, intone the sound OM.
3 As you hear the sound OM, imagine its connection with the brow chakra between the eyebrows.
4 Feel the vibration through your body and be aware of how everything in our world vibrates with its own frequency.

MODERATION

'For all things there is a time for going ahead,
and a time for following behind,
A time for slow breathing, and a time for fast
breathing,
A time to grow in strength and a time to decay,
A time to be up and a time to be down.
Therefore the sage avoids all extremes, excesses
and extravagances.'

Lao Tzu

MUSIC

Music affects us on many levels, from the superficial 'feel good' to the deeply personal and moving. It can calm us, stir us, even help to heal and nurture our mind, body and spirit. Make the time to go to concerts, perhaps learn to play a musical instrument, and rather than watch television in the evenings listen consciously to some music: how does it affect you? Let your imagination and visual powers come into play by conjuring up pictures to fit the music. Sing or dance with the music, let yourself go and leave your prejudices and inhibitions behind. Express yourself in new ways, unleashing your creativity and powers to recuperate and regenerate.

'Music can express the mystical experience better than language; it can tell of its mystery, joy, sadness and peace far better than words can utter. The fatigued intellect finds a tonic and the harassed emotions find comfort in music.'

Paul Brunton

'Music washes away from the soul the dust of everyday life.'

Berthold Auerbach

'It is not necessary to understand music; it is only necessary that one enjoy it.'

Leopold Stokowski

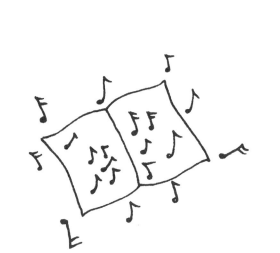

NATURE

We tend to get so caught up in the frantic pace of our lives that we forget to take delight in simple things.

The inspirational and healing power of Mother Nature is legendary. Don't ignore it: smell the flowers, repot a household plant, go for a walk in the hills or a plunge in the sea. Take yourself away from the polluted stresses of urban life and lose yourself in the beauty of nature – and encourage your children to do the same.

'Let Nature be your teacher.'

William Wordsworth

'If you have a loaf sell half and buy a lily.'

Proverb

'Before green apples blush,
Before green nuts embrown,
Why, one day in the country
Is worth a month in town.'

Christina Rossetti

'I frequently tramped eight or ten miles through
the deepest snow to keep an appointment with a
beech tree, or a yellow birch, or an old acquaintance
among the pines.'

Henry David Thoreau

PAIN

'Pain in life is inevitable, but misery is optional.'

'Troubles are often the tools by which God fashions us for better things.'

Henry Ward Beecher

'A gem cannot be polished without friction, nor a person perfected without trials.'

Pain is often a cry for help. It tells us when our body is in need of attention. If we did not feel pain we would not know when to remove our hand from something that is burning hot, or when to slow down and take care of ourselves. If your body is trying to tell you something, listen.

PRESENT MOMENT LIVING

The most precious moment you are ever going to have is this one, NOW! You can never have it again, once it is gone it is gone forever, except in your memory. At one talk I was giving a lady from the audience said, 'I can only ever be happy in retrospect: I never know I am enjoying myself at the time'. At first this sounds amusing, then sad.

To get the most out of anything we need to slow down and savour what is going on inside us and around us. A friend of my daughter was getting married and I happened to bump into her. I asked if she would mind if I gave her some advice. I suggested that during the reception she take a few moments to breathe, slow down, observe and take it all in – then later to do the same thing, but this time with her husband, then again with her mother. Just to stop and soak it all in through our senses and enjoy it for a few moments can be really wonderful.

The Precious Present

Once there was a happy and carefree young boy who was told by an old man that the Precious Present would make anyone who received it happy for ever. As he grew older the boy often wondered what this present was and who would give it to him. He thought it might be a flying carpet, hidden treasure or a magic ring. Eventually he became angry with the old man when he told him the Precious Present was a gift only he could give himself. He packed his bags and went to look for it. Many years later he returned, unhappy and ill. He was so tired of looking for the Precious Present that he simply stopped looking.

Then he realized that the Precious Present was just that. The PRESENT. Not the past, nor the future. In an instant he was happy, but he realized how much he had lost fruitlessly searching for the Precious Present, missing out on what each day had to offer. He resolved to stay in the present, knowing that he would be happy forever because forever is always the present.

Author unknown

'It doesn't matter where we live as long as we live where we are.'

'Learning moment by moment to be free in our minds and hearts, we make freedom possible for everyone the world over.'

Sonia Johnson

'If we are truly in the present moment, and are not being carried away by our thoughts and fantasies, then we are in a position to be free of fate and available to our destiny.'

Reshad Field

'Healthy people live neither in the past nor in the future. They live in the present, in the now, which gives the now a flavour of eternity because no shadows fall across it.'

Deepak Chopra

PRIORITIES

'It seems to me that the greatest stumbling block in life is this constant struggle to reach, to achieve, to acquire.'

Krishnamurti

It is all too easy to get caught up in the daily round of sleeping, eating and working without stopping to think about what it is you're aiming for. The next holiday, the next purchase, the next house – what is next on your shopping list? Is this the way you imagined your life would be when you were a teenager and full of dreams? Take a moment to reflect on what drives you, your motivations and priorities. Ask yourself if there are elements of your life that could be calmer, more focused, less 'driven'.

'Meditations Whilst Flying a Kite'

If I had my life to live over
I'd dare to make more mistakes next time,
Next time I'd relax, I would limber up
I would be sillier than I have been this trip,
I know of very few things I would take seriously.
I would laugh more and moan less.
I would take more chances.
I would climb more mountains, swim more rivers
*   and watch more sunsets.*
I would watch less TV and have more picnics.
*I would have only **actual** troubles and very few*
*   **imaginary** ones.*
I would regret my mistakes, but not go on feeling
*   guilty about them.*
I would tell people that I like them and I would
*   touch my friends.*
I would forgive others for being human and
*   I would hold no grudges.*
I would play with more children and listen to
*   more old people.*

I would go after what I wanted without believing
   *I **needed** it*
And I wouldn't place such a great value on
   accumulating wealth.
You see, I'm one of those people who lived cautiously,
   sensibly and sanely,
Hour after hour, day after day.
Oh, I've had my moments…
And if I had it to do over again I'd have more
   of them.
In fact, I'd have nothing else. Just moments, one
   after another…
Instead of living so many years ahead of each day.
I have been one of those people who never go
   anywhere without a thermometer, a hot water
   bottle, a raincoat and a parachute.
If I had to do it over again, I would travel lighter
   than I have.
If I had my life to live over again I would start
   barefoot earlier in the Spring
And stay that way later into the Fall.

I would go to more dances.
I would ride more merry-go-rounds.
And I'd pick more daisies.'

Original written by Nadine Stair
when she was 86, shortly before her death
Adapted by Tanya Wheway

PURPOSE

'A purpose is not something you create; it is something you discover.'

John-Roger

'Laziness may appear attractive, but work gives satisfaction.'

Anne Frank

Look at your life, what you have done so far and where you have come to. How would you describe it in positive terms? Can you spot an underlying purpose? A purpose in life is not a set of goals, it is rather the way you follow through your goals, it goes beyond goals. Once you have discovered what your purpose is use it as a guiding light to focus your decisions.

QI

This is an ancient Chinese term, pronounced 'chee' for which we in the West have no direct translation, but its meaning is akin to energy, life-force, spirit, or – ultimately – oneness with the universe. The Japanese have a similar word, Ki, and the Indian word is 'prana'. All Oriental practices, and their modern equivalents today, from acupressure to zen and from judo to macrobiotic eating, have as their essential aim to increase the flow of qi in the body.

QIGONG

Pronounced 'Chee Gung', this is the practice of certain energy-enhancing exercises, and is used today by millions of Chinese as a method of healing and maintaining health. It is not something that can be learnt quickly: it takes time and years of practice. The exercises are a combination of breathing, meditation, movement and body positioning, and aim to open up a channel between your body and the energy in the world around you. There are many different styles of Qigong, but it is becoming popular in the West and you should be able to find a teacher locally.

Cleansing your energy

1. Stand with your feet shoulder width apart, arms hanging relaxed at your sides, eyes closed. Clear your mind and relax.

2. As you breathe in, raise your arms up slowly out to the sides, palms upwards, until they are over your head, shoulder width apart. Turn the palms over so that they face towards the sky. Breathe out.

3. Breathe in and with your mind draw the energy of the sun, moon and heavens into your palms so that they become full with energy. Breathe in until you feel they are 'loaded'.

4. As you breathe out, use this fresh energy to clear out any negative energy inside you. Turn your palms to face down. Bring your hands slowly down and with your mind, radiate the fresh energy from your palms down the length of your body from the top of your head to the soles of your feet. Send it 3 feet into the ground, away from your personal energy field. Repeat this exercise several times.

'When we, as individuals, first rediscover our spirit, we are usually drawn to nurture and cultivate this awareness.'

Shakti Gawain

'I loafe and invite my soul.'

Walt Whitman

'Be still and silent and let the soul be a steady light which burns in a shelter where no winds blow.'

'Only when one is connected to one's own core is one connected to others ... and for me, the core, the inner spring, can best be found through solitude.'

Anne Morrow

REFLECTION

Moments of stillness and solitude are essential for healing pain and illness and for recharging batteries. People who are too busy for quiet times are often the most stressed people we know. Our busy lives mean that we often neglect ourselves. Allow yourself space to think, read, listen to music, do some of the exercises in this book, and sleep.

I love that song from *Oliver*, 'I am re-view-ing the situation'. Look objectively at what is happening in your life, take stock of where you are now, where you'd like to be going, what changes you'd like to make and how. It's not a self-indulgent luxury, it's a necessity for a healthy mind and body. Meditation, contemplation and thoughtfulness are quiet moments in which to free our minds. People often find that it is at these moments that solutions to problems arise, or new ideas surface which have been hidden by the clutter in our minds. Just as our bodies require food, physical activity and sleep to nurture and develop them, so our spirit requires 'quiet time'. So STOP, BE STILL AND REFLECT.

RELIGION

*'Some folks carry their religion on their shoulders
like a burden, instead of in their hearts like a song.'*

Some of the most atrocious crimes in past and recent history have been and are being carried out in the name of religion. However, there is a great deal we can learn from religious teachings, whatever doctrine one follows. Whatever religion we say we belong to is not as important as the way we actually live our lives. I'm sure we all know many prejudiced and uncharitable people who regularly attend religious services as well as very kind and loving people who never go to church.

RIGHT AND WRONG

'There is no right way to do the wrong thing.'

*'If thy trouble is in good works, know the trouble
will pass and the good works remain; if thy pleasure
is in sin, know the pleasure will pass and the sin
remain.'*

'He is happiest, be he king or peasant, who finds peace in his home.'

Goethe

'My whole life, in one sense, has been an experiment in how to be a portable sanctuary – learning to practice the presence of God in the midst of the stresses and strains of contemporary life.'

Richard J. Foster

'When the lamps in the house are lighted, it is like the flowering of the lotus on the lake.'

SANCTUARIES

We all need safe havens where we feel secure, loved, nurtured and uplifted. Usually these are our homes and gardens, but they can be a favourite chair, a coffee shop, a health centre, a park or a church. They can take the form of a loved person, an animal, a piece of music or a book, or the comfort of a familiar routine. You know what they are from the sense of relief and harmony when you return to them.

The most important thing is that your home should be a sanctuary from the hustle and bustle of life. Make a conscious effort to create a harmonious and balanced home. Choose restful colours, attractive plants and lighting that provides atmosphere and can be changed to suit your mood or activity. Carefully arrange furniture to be comfortable and inviting. Have plenty of cupboards so you can free your rooms of clutter. Candles, crystals, small table fountains and fresh flowers, can relax the mind, energize the body and lift the spirit. You might like to explore feng shui to ensure that the subtle energies of your home are in balance, and that there are no sharp corners or 'dead zones'.

'When one is estranged from oneself, then one is estranged from others too.'

Anne Morrow Lindberg

'What the superior person seeks is in himself; what the smaller person seeks is in others.'

Confucius

'Knowing others is wisdom. Knowing yourself is superior wisdom.'

Lao Tzu

'The delights of self-discovery are always available.'

Gail Sheehy

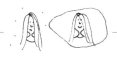

SELF-KNOWLEDGE

The longest and most important relationship of your life is the one you have with yourself, and you will never have happy, balanced relationships with others if you are out of kilter with yourself. There are today a wealth of courses, therapists and books which allow you to explore yourself, your personality, your past, your goals and desires. It can be a fascinating voyage of discovery, but beware over-indulgence in yourself for that too can prevent you from forming healthy relationships.

As a start towards self-knowledge, self-acceptance, and personal growth answer these questions:

- What is important to me?
- What are my values?
- What are my strengths?
- What are the areas I would like to improve?

SELF-WORTH

'Since you are like no other being ever created since the beginning of time, you are incomparable.'
                                        Brenda Ueland

'If you really do put a small value upon yourself, rest assured the world will not raise the price.'

'To enjoy a lifetime of romance – fall in love with yourself.'

It is so important that you value yourself as a truly unique and special person. Build a strong, healthy, respecting relationship with yourself and then you will be able to build good, strong, lasting relationships with others. When you believe in yourself and take care of yourself you have so much more to give to others.

'*Men are taught to apologize for their weaknesses,
women for their strengths.*'

Lois Wyse

SERENITY

'Serenity is an inner peace that is present even in difficult surroundings.'

William V. Pietsch

'People are like stained-glass windows. They sparkle and shine when the sun is out, but when the darkness sets in their true beauty is revealed only if there is light from within.'

Elizabeth Kubler-Ross

'In the race to be better or best, do not miss the joy of being.'

SOUL

'Fortune lost, nothing lost; courage lost, much lost; honour lost, more lost; soul lost, all lost.'

'Thus at the centre of the self there is a hole and a mystery. Our own soul is unknown to us,'

'To seek the nature of the soul, we must premise that the soul is defined as the first principle of life.'
Thomas Aquinas

'There is nothing on earth so curious for beauty or so absorbent of it as a soul.'
Wassily Kandinsky

'Let us be grateful to people who make us happy;
they are the charming gardeners who make our souls
blossom.'

Marcel Proust

SUCCESS

'To laugh often and love much,
To win the respect of intelligent persons and
    the affection of children;
To earn the approbation of honest critics
And to endure the betrayal of false friends;
To appreciate beauty; to find the best in others;
To give one's self;
To leave the world a bit better, whether by a healthy
    child, a garden patch or a redeemed social
    condition;
To have played and laughed with enthusiasm and
    sung with exultation;
To know even one life has breathed easier because
    you have lived
This is to have succeeded.'

Ralph Waldo Emerson

'To be successful the first thing to do is fall in love with your work.'

Sister Mary Lauretta

T'AI CHI

T'ai Chi is an oriental system of simple movements which create body strength and inner harmony, and is often referred to as 'moving meditation'. The circular and spiralling movements look slow but do in fact develop suppleness and strength. Although it is a form of self-defence, it is also practised for its health benefits. It allows energy to flow through the meridians in the body, healing energy blockages, or stagnant qi.

Warm up Technique

1 Stand with your feet slightly more than shoulder width apart, knees bent, spine straight.
2 Keeping feet stuck to the floor, push with the left leg and feel it turn your waist to the right.
3 When your body weight is 70% over the right leg, release the coiled power by pushing with your right leg. Feel it turn your waist around to the left, until the left leg compresses.
4 Repeat the movements, keeping relaxed, loose and level.

Rooting Exercise

1 Physically sink your body weight and imagine that it is in your lower belly and legs.
2 Grip the ground with your feet like claws, while pushing the legs against the ground and each other. This pushing turns the hips, waist and belly from side to side.

TIME

'Gather ye rosebuds while ye may.'

'This job is killing me but I'm making so much money I can afford it.'

Time is one of our most precious commodities, if not the most, so we must look to use it in the most productive and enjoyable way. My dream is that we can all actually create something worthwhile, take much out of life and yet put much back in – while having fun!

Keep checking your priorities. Imagine you only have one month left to live. What would you choose to do or complete in the time you have left to you? Who would you spend it with? How would you judge the success of your life? Write your obituary and your epitaph. Then consider this: are you happy with the way your life is going or are there some priorities you need to shift?*

* The Sanctuary offers courses on life planning.

Take Time for Twelve Things

✧ Take time to work – it is the price of success.

✧ Take time to think – it is the source of power.

✧ Take time to play – it is the secret of youth.

✧ Take time to read – it is the foundation of knowledge.

✧ Take time to worship – it is the highway of reverence and washes the dust of the earth from our eyes.

✧ Take time to help and enjoy friends – it is the source of happiness.

✧ Take time to love – it is the sacrament of life.

✧ Take time to dream – it hitches the soul to the stars.

✧ Take time to laugh – it is the singing that helps with life's load.

✧ Take time for beauty – it is everywhere in nature.

✧ Take time for health – it is the true wealth and treasure of life.

✧ Take time to plan – it is the secret of being able to have time to take time for the first 11 things!

'More things are wrought by prayer than this world dreams of.'

Alfred Lord Tennyson

VISUALIZATION

Visualization is a focused form of imagination: in a way a form of praying. Some people use it to amass material goods or improve their confidence, or to assist the body in healing itself. It can also be used as a relaxation technique. Read this guided visualization several times over until you can remember it clearly. Lie on the floor and let it flow in your imagination … it will relax and refresh you.

'Your body is heavy and relaxed … your joints are soft, your muscles warm and relaxed, your shoulders and hips feel heavy and open. Your head is heavy on the floor and your face is soft. Your hands and feet are soft and relaxed. Your spine is releasing more and more. Your breathing is coming and going lightly and steadily in its own rhythm. Your throat is passive and relaxed, and your mind is empty. You are walking along a path towards a walled garden. There is a gate into the garden, and you are walking towards the gate. Go through the gate into the beautiful garden. The sun is deliciously warm on your body, and you soak up the warmth…

In the garden are beautiful flowers and shrubs all around you. Butterflies are dancing in the sunlight. You can smell the lovely scents arising from the warm flowers and you wander among the flower beds enjoying the colours, the shapes, the perfumes…

The sun is warm, it is peaceful, quiet and sleepy, just the occasional murmuring of bees or birdsong arises from time to time in the silence…

In the middle of the garden is a pool of clear, clean water. You walk to the pool and dip yourself into the clear, clean, sparkling water. All your tiredness, sadness and confusion is washed away in the crystal water of the pool.

Come out of the pool fresh and clean, newly born, and lay yourself down to dry in the warm sunshine, surrounded by the beauty of the garden …'

Paddy O'Brien

WISDOM

Developing wisdom is a continuous process of learning about life, which, like an incomplete jigsaw puzzle is never clear to us in all its entirety. Thinking about who we are as individuals and as human beings is a start, as is viewing the world in both an optimistic and realistic light.

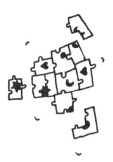

'Be wiser than other people if you can, but do not tell them so.'

'A good man says no slowly; a wise man says no at once.'

'What is the point of life if we do not learn from wise men of old?'

Katrina Graham

'Joy helps us heighten our level of consciousness so we can more readily tap our inner wisdom.'

Charlotte Davis Kasl

'Wisdom and wholeness deepen in us when we reflectively allow ideas and feelings to sit inside us for a while.'

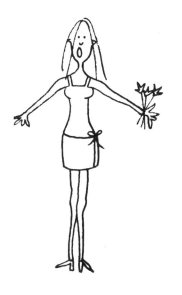

WONDERMENT

'If a child is to keep alive his inborn sense of wonder without any such gift from the fairies, he needs the companionship of at least one adult who can share it, rediscovering with him the joy, excitement, and mystery of the world we live in.'

'To see the world in a grain of sand,
And heaven in a wild flower;
Hold infinity in the palm of your hand,
And eternity in an hour.'

William Blake

'We were gone almost a month and everything was sensual. Everything was erotic. It's a gift of travel, where everything is infused with meaning, compressed so you begin to see the golden strand that weaves life together. You are in a constant state of awe.'

Terry Williams

YIN AND YANG

In oriental philosophies, yin and yang express the 'wholeness' of nature, the order inherent in nature, the combination of complementary yet opposing forces. Thus: day and night, joy and sadness, love and hate, masculine and feminine, hot and cold. Plants (yin) convert carbon dioxide to oxygen; animals (yang) convert oxygen to carbon dioxide. Our bodies are also governed by yin and yang energies, so we need to try to live in harmony with the natural world, adapting to each season and eating food consistent with our particular constitution.

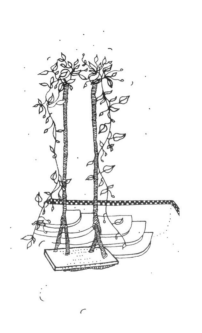

YOGA

The practice of yoga is a fusion of the physical and the spiritual, with calm yet powerful postures and movements which stretch the body's muscles and give a sense of inner peace, harmony and oneness. Incorrect postures, developed over a lifetime of sitting with our legs crossed, slumping in front of the television, or carrying heavy shopping deplete our energy and cause health problems. As we slow down our normal activities we get in touch with a deeper reality and seem to cast off petty everyday concerns.

Breathing plays a key role in yoga, and the exercises, if practised regularly, can be carried on into advanced years, bringing benefit to the mind, body and spirit.

Think deeply
Speak gently
Love much
Laugh often
Work hard
Give freely
Pay promptly
Pray earnestly
And be kind

The Sanctuary in Covent Garden is a Day Spa and Fitness Club exclusively for women owned and operated by The Sanctuary Spa Group, a company founded originally as Wheway Lifestyle International by Tanya and Allan Wheway in 1989. The Sanctuary Spa Group have recently opened Sanctuary Spas in David Lloyd Clubs located in Sidcup, Stevenage, Chigwell, Milton Keynes, Leeds and Manchester. A Sanctuary Spa and Fitness Club is located in the Lake District within Rank's Oasis Holiday Village and the latest to open is a Sanctuary Health Club and Spa within the new Kensington Hotel, London. All of these Sanctuary Spas welcome men as well as women.

The Sanctuary Spa Group provide worldwide consultancy in the spa business and created and commissioned the award-winning Chiva-Som health resort in Thailand. They are soon to open their first Sanctuary abroad on the Dead Sea in Jordan and have recently launched a range of Sanctuary Spa products and their first CD.

THE SANCTUARY

Covent Garden, London

A DAY SPA EXCLUSIVELY

FOR WOMEN

Contact:

The Sanctuary
12 Floral Street
Covent Garden
London
WC2E 9DH

Telephone: 0171 420 5151
Fax: 0171 497 0410

for details of day and evening rates and treatments available.